Drymen and Buchanan:
A Further Selection
of Old Photographs

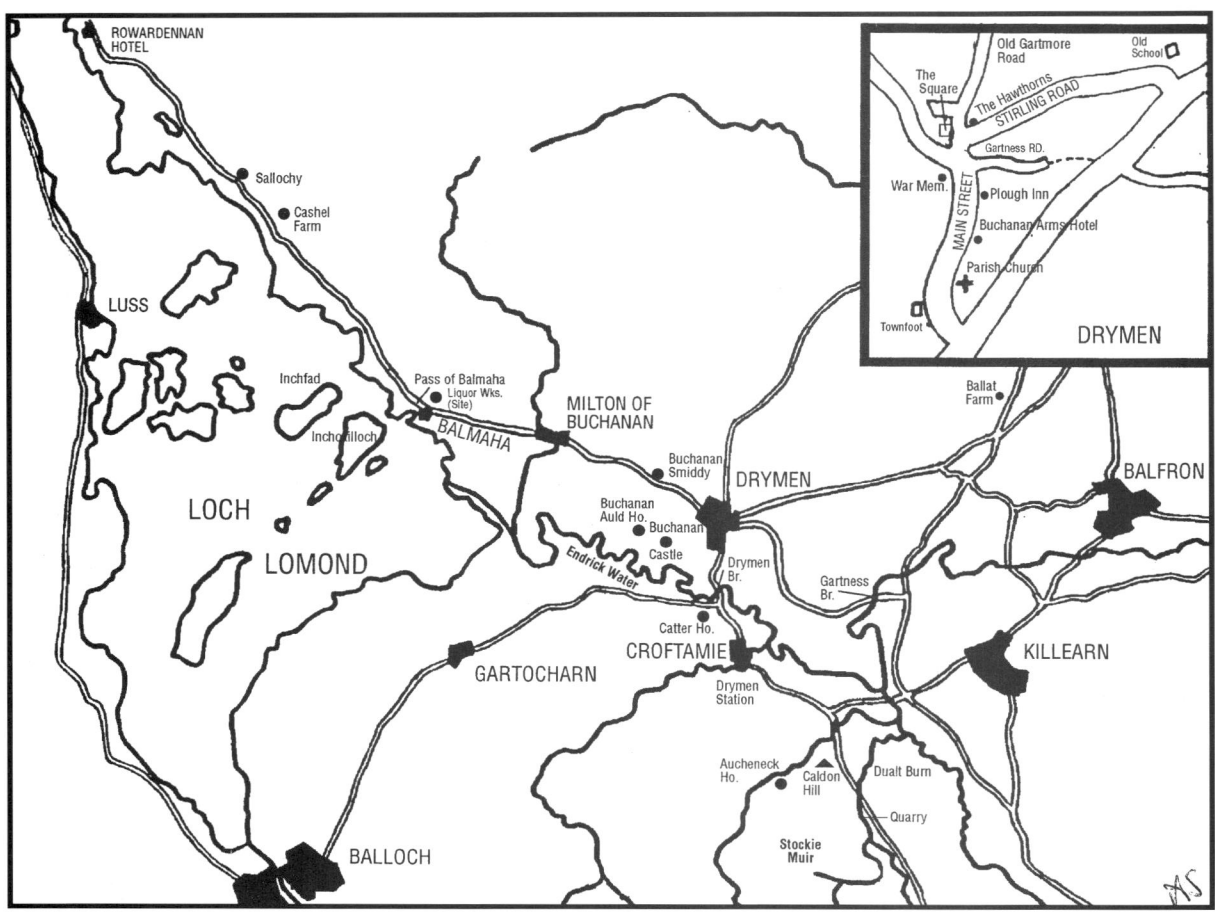

Front cover   Looking south to the Campsie Hills from Riskhead (Townhead), Old Gartmore Road, Drymen. From a 19th century painting by Dr James Beveridge (by courtesy of Mrs Margaret Kirk)

Back Cover   An aerial view of the ruins of Buchanan Castle which was demolished in 1954; only the walls remain. (Photo by M. B. Bruce).

DRYMEN AND BUCHANAN:

A FURTHER SELECTION

OF OLD PHOTOGRAPHS

By

Mary B. Bruce

STIRLING DISTRICT LIBRARIES

First published 1993

STIRLING
DISTRICT COUNCIL

ISBN 1 8705422 2 3

Published by
Stirling District Libraries
Stirling

Printed by
Cordfall Ltd
041 332 4640

ACKNOWLEDGEMENTS

By sharing valuable old photographs, many friends give a great deal of pleasure to all of us, in addition to the help and time which they have contributed. This is their book. My sincere thanks to all who have helped in many ways:-

Mrs. H. Aitken
Mr. T. Anderson
Mrs. K. Atherton
Mrs. N. Brown
Mrs. A Cameron
Mrs. A. Elder
Mrs. S. Forbes
Mr. A. Fraser, Balfron
Mr. John Goodwin
Mr. P. Johnson
Mrs. M. Kirk
Mr. Alex Lees

Mac Images for the map
Mrs. J. Mason, Jun.
Mr N. Mason
Mrs. M. McCallum
Mr. D. C. McCallum
Mr. O. McDonald
Mr. A. McGregor
Mr. & Mrs. J. McQueen
Mr. J. Mitchell
Mr. S. Shearlaw
Mr. W. Simpson
Mr. G. Turner

I am specially indebted to Alison Brown for advising, editing and always being particularly helpful.

Mary B. Bruce

To Readers

The spelling of some place names has changed over the years. That of the current Ordnance Survey Map is the one of choice.

A note of caution! If you are tempted to visit old buildings featured in this book, you are reminded that private ground should be visited only with the owner's consent.

Anyone with information and old photographs of the district which would be of interest to Drymen and District Local History Society and are willing to lend them for copying, please contact:

Mrs. Alison Brown
Community Librarian
Drymen Library
The Square, Drymen
G63 0BL
Telephone: 0360-60751.

MAIN St. DRYMEN.

1. MAIN STREET, DRYMEN IN THE 1920s

Looking north to the Hawthorns at the beginning of this century. In the centre of the picture at the edge of the road is a communal stoup (water hydrant). The Plough Inn is the single-storey building on the right.

2. THE SQUARE, DRYMEN IN THE 1920s

The War Memorial was dedicated in 1920. Beyond it was Primrose Bank demolished in 1974 when the new Balmaha Road was built. In the centre is Hillside the home for many years of the Waddell family and occupied by Mrs. N. Frame (née Waddell). Parked in front of the Clachan Inn is Dick's bus (of Croftamie), the first to run between Drymen and Glasgow. The hardness of the wooden seats and the shaking of the bus made the journey very uncomfortable.

3. ARMISTICE SERVICE AT DRYMEN WAR MEMORIAL, 1946

In front: Mrs. Sweet (with umbrella), G. Gilfillan (officer)

Front Row Facing: John Vickers, L. Campbell, A. 'Tuck' Angus, D. McTavish, J. Bilsland, J. Gray, D. Lawson, W. Davidson, John Goodwin, A. MacFarlane, G. Goodwin, X unnamed.

Row Behind Includes: B. Anderson, J. Strachan, D. Johnson, F. Billett, J. Mason Sen., J. 'Bing' Angus, N. Sweet, J. Friar, A. Stewart, J. Angus Sen. (with bowler), James Goodwin, J. McAlpine.

Back Row: Miss Gilfillan, J. Elder, Mrs. McLean Kirk, Dr. Maud MacKinnon (inside gate at the Hawthorns).

4

4. RANKIN'S BUS SERVICE

This Thornycroft Bus, parked at Kirk's Shop, Drymen, ran from Aberfoyle to Glasgow via Drymen from 1920.

The driver was Mr. George Fraser (Alex's brother) and his conductress, Miss Hannah Stewart.

5. STEAM ROAD ROLLER AT THE HAWTHORNS, DRYMEN

This was a common sight over fifty years ago. Due to the scarcity of traffic on the road, its slow speed in no way inconvenienced the motorist. The strong smell of melted tar when the roads were being repaired, was supposed to ease whooping cough and respiratory infections. The 'tarry' boiler accompanied the road roller. The Plough Inn in the centre background is now the Salmon Leap Hotel.

The 'pumpstones' on the right are still there, though hidden by shrubs.

5

6. STIRLING ROAD, DRYMEN, FROM THE SQUARE.

In the centre right is Ashdale, 6 Stirling Road, the home and grocer's shop in the 1870s of Mr. Wm. Liddell whose son James was apprenticed as a draper in Stirling. He later became a congregational minister and in 1989 went as a missionary to Mongolia. Eric, his second son, was born in China in 1902. In 1907 the family returned to Drymen and stayed at Ashbank, Old Balmaha Road. Eric attended Drymen School until the autumn of 1908 when he went with his brother Rob to the School for Missionaries in London.

On the *left* of the picture is the Hollybush Tearoom and Mrs. Robertson's antique shop behind which her son James had a workshop in the early 1920s where he designed, and with the help of Mr. Ronnie Mason, built the first Cowal car. The original engine, a four-cylinder two stroke, is in Glasgow's Museum of Transport.

7. ERIC HENRY LIDDELL, B.Sc., 1902-1945

A man with a deep-rooted Christian faith who is remembered for giving up the chance of an Olympic Gold Medal in the 100 metres in Paris in 1924 because he would not run on a Sunday. He then surprised everyone by going on to win a Gold in the 400 metres. The year after he graduated at Edinburgh University he turned his back on the rewards of Olympic fame to serve as his father before him, as a missionary in northern China. Eric died of an inoperable brain tumour in 1945 in a Japanese Internment Camp at Weihsien.

In 1981 the film 'Chariots of Fire' was made telling the story of this caring hero, conscientious and consistent in his spiritual beliefs.

7

8

8. DRYMEN SCHOOL PUPILS IN 1892

Back Row: Will Forrest, Jimmy Graham, Mr. John Hall, Pate Moir, Archie Billett.

Middle Row: Watt McAdam, Joe Henry, Beth Roy (daughter of the Rev. John Roy), Jean Osborne, Alex Fraser, J. Bilsland.

Front Row: Meg Tully, Mary McFarlane, Lizzie McAdam, Kate McCaig, Annie McCaig and Mary Gilfillan.

Mr. Hall was appointed headmaster at Drymen in May 1891 when Mr. Duncan Stewart retired. Mr. Hall taught previously at Hutcheson's Grammar School, Glasgow.

9. DRYMEN PRIMARY SCHOOL, 1928

Back Row: Miss Stewart, I. Campbell, James Goodwin, J. McLay, J. Adamson, W. McAllister, A. McGregor, A. Clark, Mr. Abercrombie, Headmaster.

Middle Row: Unnamed, D. Kirk, C. Fisher, I. Vickers, M. Begg, A. McLay, W. Vickers.

Front Row: G. Turner, B. Monteith, B. Anderson, F. Goodwin, E. Aitchison, H. McGregor, M. Forrest, T. McLay.

11. DRYMEN PRIMARY SCHOOL, 1952

Back Row: Mr. Tait (headmaster), A. Elder, J. Gibson, M. McKay, V. Stewart, D. Brown, M. McDougall, D. McAinsh, H. Veitch, M. Murray, C. Murray, M. Aitchison, B. McGregor, P. Gibb, Miss Aitken (teacher).

Second Row: J. Strachan, G. McDougall,
J. McIntosh, J. Angus,
A. Murray, N. McCallum,
J. Morrison, B. Tait, G. Lees,
A. Brand, C. McKay, I. Hay.

Third Row: I. McTavish, A. Ross, C. Shields,
C. McKay, V. Lawson,
S. Angus, C. Angus, G. Taylor,

G. Gibson, A. Mason, K. Strachan,
P. Aitchison, A. Gorman,
A. McKay.

Front Row: I. McCallum, I. Fergus, J. McCallum,
D. Kirk, G. Angus, W. Kirk,
D. Holmes, D. Strachan, Unnamed,
A. Lees, C. Johnson.

11

10

10. DRYMEN SCHOOL PUPILS 1937-1938

Back Row: Unnamed, K. Black, T. Anderson, J. Calder, S. Eccles, - McLaren, D. Webster.

Next Row: M. Mason, B. Anderson, F. Aitchison, A. Anderson, S. Dunlop, E. Campbell, E. Black.

Seated: J. Mason, D. McCallum, B. Anderson, E. Eccles, I. Aitchison, P. Wilson, I. MacLean, P. Calder.

Front Row: T. Lindsay, F. Dunlop and J. Elder. The headmaster was Mr. Wilson and his assistant Miss Aitken.

12. MILLSKITE, DRYMEN, 1903

The house on the right in the Gartness Road was the home of the McCallum family for three generations. It is known now as Millburn, renovated and extended by the present owner, Mr. Graham Johnstone. On the extreme left was Primrose Bank now demolished and on its right The Hawthorns.

13. THE OLD BRIDGE AT GARTNESS

The old bridge over the Endrick at Gartness connected the parishes of Drymen and Killearn and was built in 1715. It was replaced by a modern iron bridge in 1971 and this lovely old bridge was demolished.

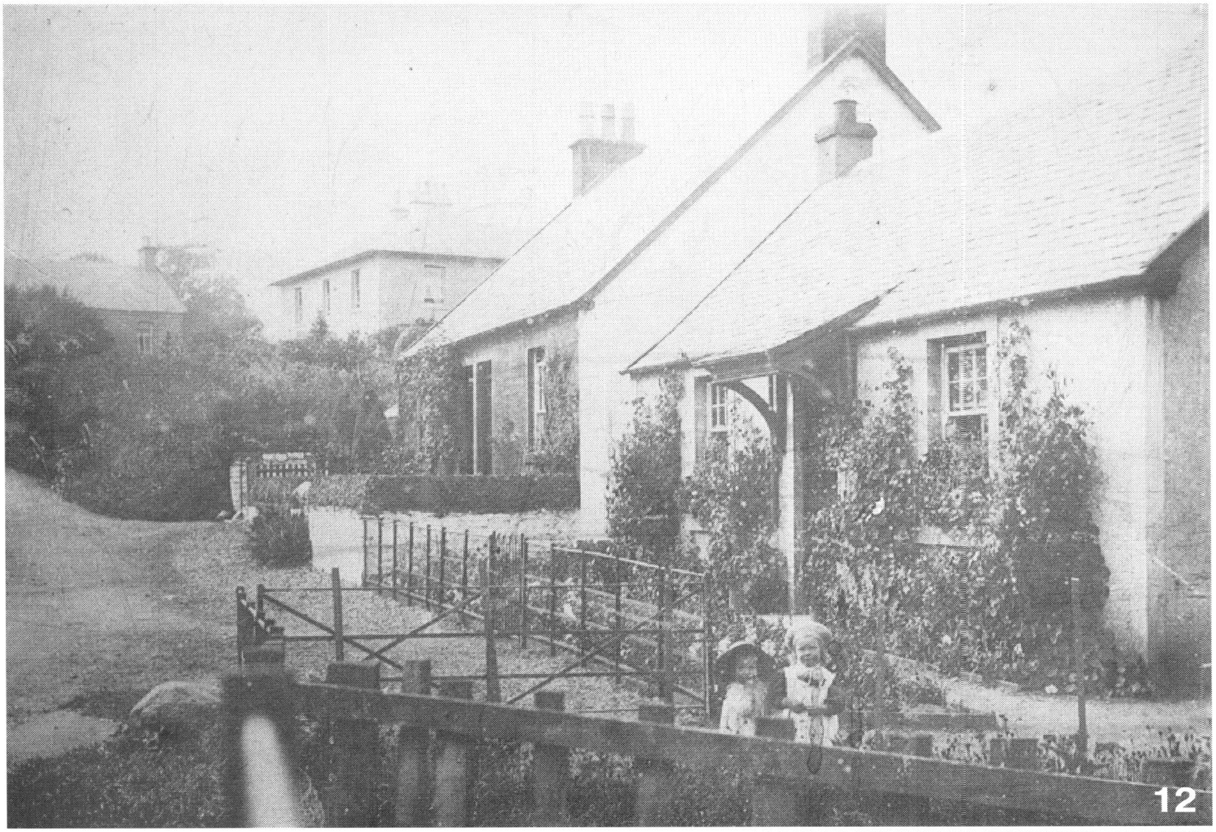
12

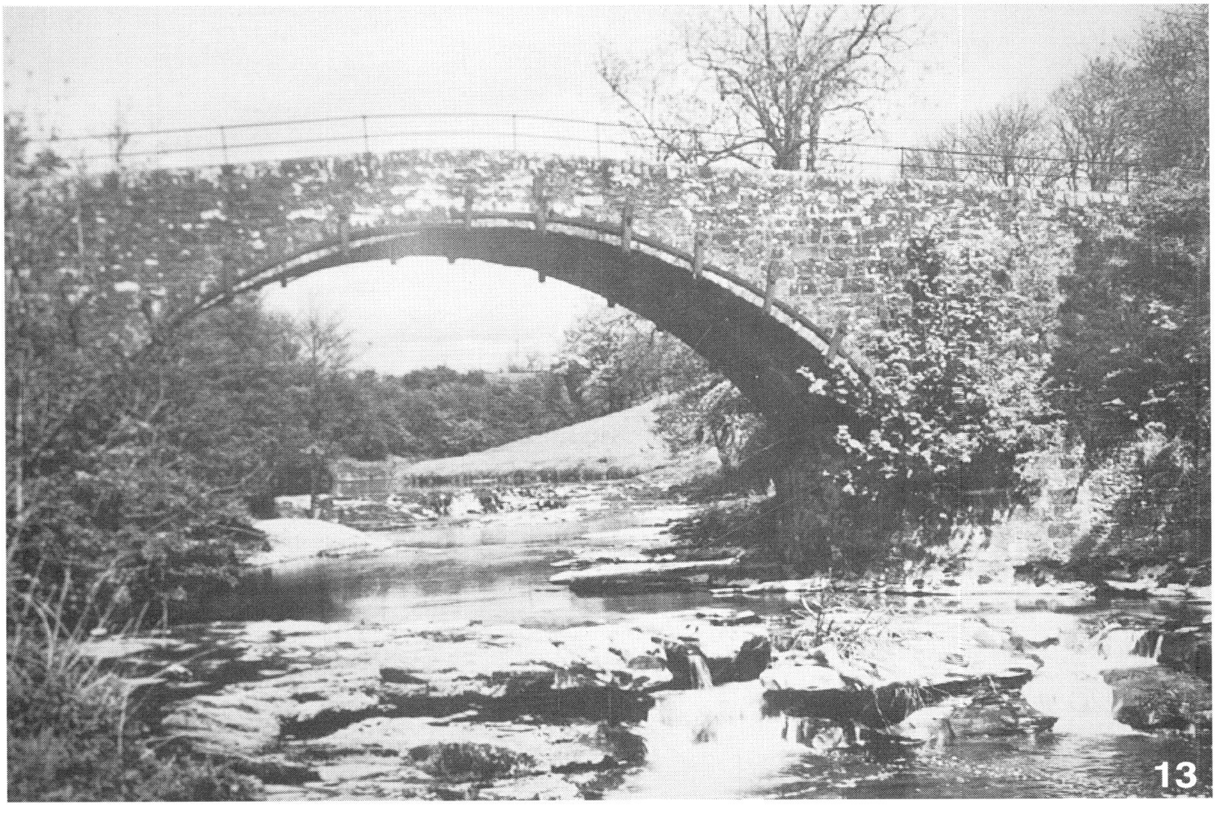
13

14. KITCHEN RANGE, MAIN STREET, DRYMEN, 1890s

This range, in the home of the Lyle family, kept the rooms warm, supplied constant hot water both in the side boiler and in the large cast iron kettle and all cooking and baking was done on it.

Mr. Archie Lyle who lived there as a boy, came back from Seattle, U.S.A. in 1980. He brought with him some early photographs which he had treasured since he emigrated as a young man. This was one of them.

15. SCHOOLFRIENDS, DRYMEN, IN THE EARLY 1920s

Left to Right *Standing*: Jock McGregor, Fanny Binnie, John McCaig, Chrissie Corrigan and Walter Vickers.

Kneeling: Lizzie Doey and Nellie Vickers (Mrs. Brown).

16

16. DRYMEN 10TH STIRLINGSHIRE GIRL GUIDE COMPANY, 1922

The Drymen Girl Guide Company was formed in 1918 by Miss Mabel Scott, Balfunning with two patrols, the 'Forget-me-nots' and the 'Marguerites'. In July 1922 the annual camp was held jointly with the Killearn Company at the Blair, Critreoch Bay, Loch Lomond. There were very few fine days and there was a great deal of rain. One night cows got into the store tent and ate 'four dozen bananas and a good many strawberries'.

Back row: On left is Miss Mabel Scott (Mrs. Rowley Orr).

Front row: On left is Nell Veitch (Mrs. McIntyre).

Others in the picture are: M. Graham, P. Simpson, J. Sinclair, C & M. McAuley, C. McGowan, D. Sharp, M. Graham, E. Morrison, J. Paterson and D. Simpson.

17. DRYMEN W.R.I., 1973

Back Row: Mrs. McGregor, Mrs. Muir,
Mrs. E. Brown, Mrs. A. Elder,
Mrs. E. Fraser, Mrs. N. Elder,
Mrs. J. Allan, Mrs. J. McLuckie,
Mrs. A. McNally, Mrs. A. Lawson,
Mrs. C. Smith, Mrs. M. Johnson.

3rd Row: Mrs. R. Howe, Mrs. J. Mason Sen.,
Unnamed, Mrs. B. Tedstone,
Mrs. A. Ross, Mrs. C. Wyllie,
Mrs. McAinsh, Mrs. Adams,
Miss Keay, Mrs. Aucock,
Mrs. Joan White, Mrs. McLay,
Unnamed.

2nd Row: Miss. N. Hall, Mrs. Wilson,
Mrs. Craig, Mrs. Douglas,
Mrs. Chapman, Mrs. M. Kirk,
Miss Aitken, Mrs. Mailer,
Mrs. M. Gardner.

Front Row: Unnamed, Miss J. Johnston,
Mrs. M. Stratton, Mrs. M Turner,
Mrs. Steel, Mrs. Beauman,
Miss. M. McCaig, Mrs. McAdam.

18

---

18. DRYMEN UNITED FOOTBALL CLUB ANNUAL DANCE, 1930

Held in the Foresters' Hall (now Spar). And they danced to the three piece band called 'The Arcadians'.

In the group being presented with their awards are:-

Pat Lawson, Sandy McGregor,
B. MacMillan, Neil McKechnie,
John Parker, Jack Boyd,
Jock Anderson, Will Stewart,
Jock McGregor, D. Burnett,
Murdo Chisholm, Willie Kirk,
Rev. J. T. Monteith, Mr. Innes
(referee), Bob Brown,
Stevie MacMillan and
Bill Anderson.

19. DRYMEN BOYS' BRIGADE FOOTBALL ELEVEN, 1961-62

Back Row: Alwyn Lees, David Strachan, John McQueen, Douglas Bain, Ian Hay, Ian McCallum.

Front Row: Sandy Forbes, Ian Stuart, Jim Vickers, Jimmy McCallum and Charles McKay.

Their captain and trainer was Mr. Alan Ferrie of Endrickbank, Croftamie. The team was picked regularly to play in the Glasgow Select.

19

20

20. AT LOANINGHEAD FARM

Cutting a field of wheat in 1912 are 'Star', 'Darky', and 'Aberfoyle' with Mr. Tom Johnstone seated on the binder. Mr. James Turner Senior, on the left, farmed there from 1909 to 1950. His six sons are James, Robert, William, Ian, George and Alan, all farmers.

21. AT BALLAT FARM IN THE 1930s

Enjoying tea and a 'piece' during a well-earned break at the hay-making. On the right is the wooden tripod which was the central support for the hayrick.
Left to right: Ned Wallace, Oliver McDonald,
                Johnny Easton and
                George McDonald (Oliver's
                brother).
and 'Nancy' in the rake patiently awaits her piece and tea.

22

22. BUCHANAN ARMS HOTEL IN THE 1890S

The hotel was originally a small country inn with an adjacent farm, Ballanton, both owned by the Duke of Montrose and tenanted by Robert Buchanan and then James Buchanan. When the Strathendrick Farmers' Club had their annual outing, they met at the hotel prior to their departure by coach. This may have been one of these occasions.

Second from the right is the Rev. John Roy and fourth from right is Mr. William Kirk, Campbell's grandfather.

23

23. BUCHANAN ARMS HOTEL, 1936

In 1935 the hotel was purchased by Mr. David Burnett who, conditional to the Electricity Board supplying electricity to Drymen, extensively reconstructed and extended the buildings. The Hotel was again greatly improved and extended in 1982 and in 1990, when it was renamed the Buchanan Highland Hotel.

24. DRYMEN PARISH CHURCH

The present Church stands on a site which may go back to the 11th century. The burial ground contains many recumbent gravestones, one, until recently, bearing the date 1618. In 1771 the Church building was described as ruinous and unsafe, and the heritors (ie. the local landowners) asked Mr. George Taylor, a mason of Arnprior, to prepare plans for 'a plain but substantial building'. It was completed at a cost of £384 2s. 3d. Since then substantial alterations and improvements have been carried out at various times, the last in 1988-89 being the most extensive at a cost of £44,500.

The beautiful triple-light framed glass window was gifted by Mr. A. M. McQueen of Gateside in the 1880s. The Church is listed as a building of Special Architectural or Historic Interest, Category B.

25

25. THE COMMUNION CUPS THAT WERE MISLAID

From the Presbytery records of 1668 and again in 1705 and 1712 there was concern at the lack of communion silver at Drymen Parish Church. In 1732 the Kirk Session purchased Communion Cups at a cost of eleven pounds and eight shillings. In 1986, by accident, a heavy locked box was found in the Bank. When opened by a locksmith it was found to contain two silver cups each engraved 'The Communion Cup of the Kirk of Drymen 1732' and a flagon in Britannia metal inscribed 'The Kirk of Drymen 1852'. New cups had been gifted to the Church in the 1880s and no doubt for safe keeping, the original ones were lodged in the Bank and then forgotten about for a hundred years.

26. TOWNFOOT, DRYMEN

On the extreme left of this row of houses was a joiners' workshop used by Mr. McFarlane ('Putty Jock' 1840-1922) at the end of last century and the beginning of this; then by Mr. Sandy Howe until he retired in the 1970s.

27. AMERICAN SERVICEMEN AT TOWNFOOT ABOUT 1941

American servicemen, billeted in the Buchanan Arms Hotel, looking at the thatched roof of the end cottage damaged by fire. On the back of the photograph are the names of the men.

The two-storeyed house was the home of Mr. & Mrs. John Goodwin until 1939. The three two-apartment thatched dwellings were typical of the original workers' houses. The only one of this type remaining is Riskhead (also called Townhead) on the corner of the Old Balmaha Road. The house on the extreme right and partly hidden, was owned by the Buchanan Arms Hotel and for many years was the home of their head gardener, Mr. Kelly. In 1976 it was destroyed by fire and a new house was built on the site.

Left to Right: T/U C. E. Lavandrowski (Poland), New York.
Cpl. H. L. Durham, McKinney, Kentucky.
Cpl. M. A. Maceyak, Connellsville, P. A.
P.F.C. J. N. Bastion, Kingston, Michigan.

27

28. CROFTAMIE PRIMARY SCHOOL PUPILS, 1957

Croftamie School was opened in 1907 to take the place of Kilmaronock School. Sixty-four pupils were enrolled and that number was maintained for many years. When Croftamie School opened pupils came from a school at Craighat now gone and from the red sandstone school at Finnich Toll which closed in 1924 and since then has been a dwelling house.

In the photograph are:-

Back Row: Miss MacLean (headmistress), K. Brown, John Brown, P. Cunningham, A. Sweet, F. Davidson, R. Fraser, C. Law, A. Atherton.

Middle Row: S. Atherton, Jim Brown, W. Smith, J. Hillhouse, S. Brown, R. Atherton, A. Orr, L. Barr, A. Wood, G. Vickers.

Front Row: R. Hillhouse, G. Law, J. Law and D. Law.

29. CROFTAMIE W.R.I. OUTING ABOUT 1930s

In 1927 Miss Goldie, Kilmaronock Manse, called a meeting in the Old School of all interested in starting a 'Rural'. A committee was formed and Croftamie W.R.I. was inaugurated. From then on meetings have been held monthly in Croftamie School. This photograph shows members and friends at a picnic at the Mount, Balfron about the 1930s.

Back Row Standing: Mrs. Paterson, Unnamed, Mrs. Johnson (Catter), K. Jamieson (Mrs. Davidson), J. Morrison, Miss Miller, Unnamed, M. McLachlan.

Third Row Kneeling: Unnamed, Miss Gardner, M. Stewart (Mrs Hamilton), Mrs. Buchanan (Nell's mother), Unnamed, Unnamed.

Second Row: J. Harvey (Mrs Paton), Unnamed, B. Bilsland (Mrs McArthur)

Front Row: Isa Orr, Unnamed, Jean Graham, Jenny McQueen (Mrs Renfrew), M. Bilsland, N. Buchanan (Mrs Aitken), Mary Johnson.

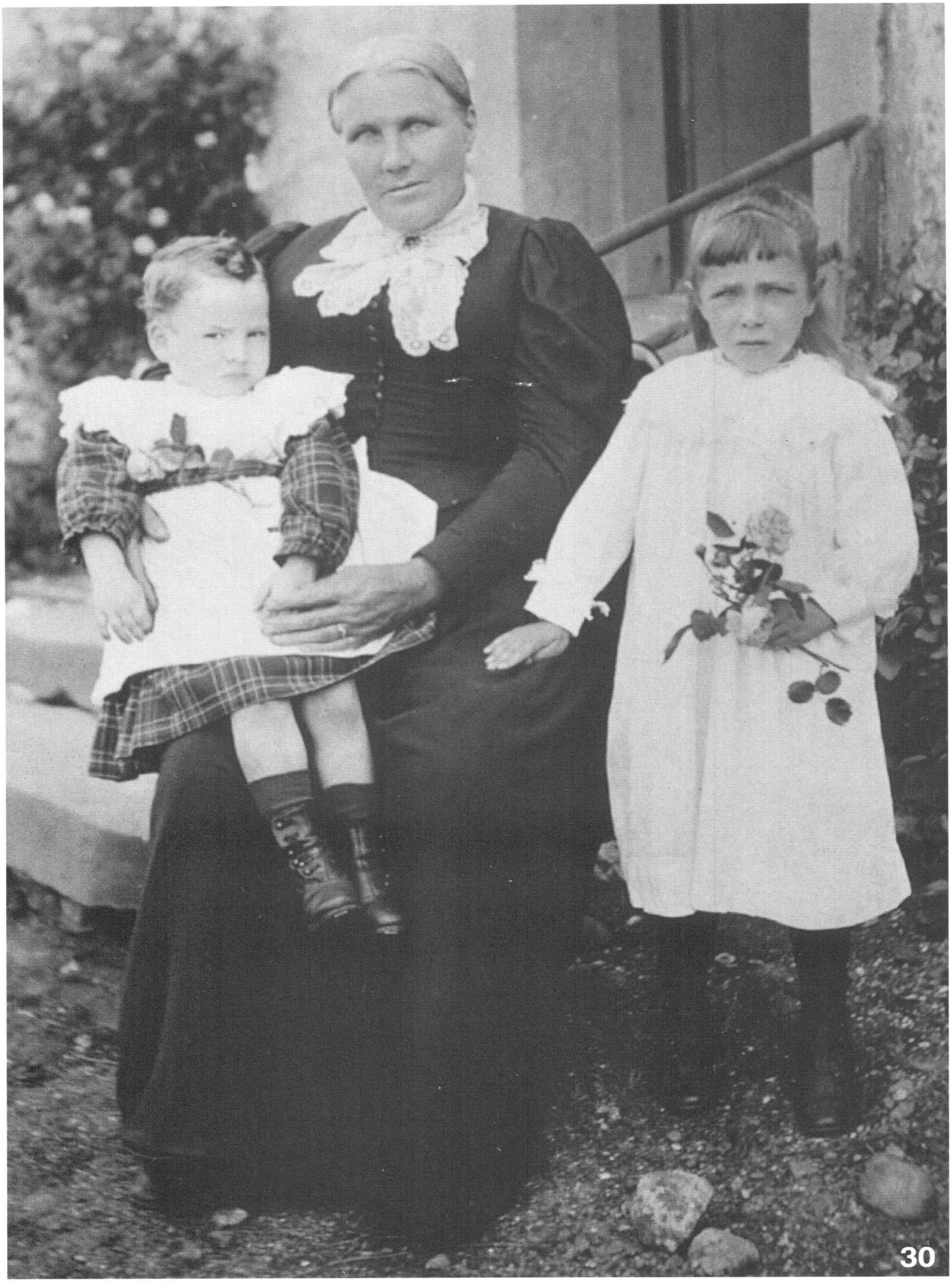

31

Pictured with her grandchildren James Brown and Jessie Stewart. Note that the boy is wearing skirts, a common practice in that era.

James Brown is on the left of photograph. No. 31, above.

Woodcutters having completed the felling of a tree which took them a whole day. With a modern chain saw it would take only a fraction of the time.

On the left is James Brown, Croftamie father of Stewart Brown. On the right is Jock McGregor of the 'Tea-pot Inn'.

34

34. SNOWSTORM ON THE STOCKIEMUIR, LOOKING TOWARDS GLASGOW

Every decade or more, destructive gales, great rainstorms and severe snowstorms caused widespread havoc. This picture of the cottages at the Dualt on the Stockiemuir road shows the severity of a snowstorm at the end of last century. The dark area to the right of the tree in the centre was a large red sandstone quarry on the Aucheneck Estate, operating in the 1830s. For four generations the McLaren family lived at West Dualt, Mr. William McLaren and his brother James working the Quarry until the early 1890s when it was finished.

A torrential rainstorm caused the Dualt Burn to change its course and flooded the quarry. All attempts to rectify matters were of no avail, though the area on the lower side of the main road is very overgrown, the outline of the quarry can still be seen.

32. MONTROSE ESTATES' LORRY

The driver is Mr. Hugh Forbes, father of Sandy and with him is Mr. Bill Maitland. Both worked for the Duke of Montrose and this lorry was used before the last war for transporting goods, mainly animal feed, from Glasgow.

The lorry could be adapted to transport sheep.

33. DRYMEN STATION, AT CROFTAMIE 1857-1957

The Forth and Clyde Railway was begun in 1856 and Drymen Station was opened the following year. this new means of transport being available to everyone, meant that local people were no longer dependent on the land for their livelihood. Every commodity, most importantly milk, was handled by the staff, consisting of the Stationmaster, two clerks, two signalmen and a boy. In the 1920s the bus service between Drymen and Glasgow was introduced and the railway journey via Balloch became less popular. As the bus service increased, the passenger trains decreased and by 1934 were discontinued. Latterly the railway service consisted of three goods trains weekly to Balloch with none from Balloch. The railway closed in 1957.

32

33

35

35. MRS. McLELLAN AND FAMILY, DUALT

Mrs. Kate McLellan seated on the right was orphaned at the age of six and was brought up by her grandmother Mrs. Catherine McLaren at the Dualt. Kate married a foreman who worked at the quarry. He died at the age of 34 and she returned to the Dualt to bring up her three daughters and later her cousin's three orphaned children. She was small of build and a hard worker. On the south side of the Caldon Hill she grew an annual crop of carrots which she marketed in the outskirts of Glasgow. She died in 1956 aged 95.

Seated next to Mrs. McLellan is her daughter, Mrs. A. McAllister, Blairmore, Drymen and the other daughter is Mrs. James MacFarlane, Balmaha.

Standing on the right is the grandfather of Mr. Alex Ferrier, Killearn.

Taking photographs then necessitated long exposures. The adults have kept still, but the three children have kept on the move, giving blurred images.

36. AUCHENECK HOUSE

Aucheneck was originally part of the Church lands of Finnich, a very old and extensive estate originally owned by the Earls of Leanox.

After many centuries and the complex joining and separating of parts, due to purchase and inheritance, Aucheneck Estate was bought in 1823 by Mr. James McNair, an outstanding land improver. He erected a red sandstone mansion house and created a beautiful estate by planting, draining, fencing and building roads, bridges and dykes. Mr. John Wilson, the next owner, continued the work of Mr. McNair and built a large addition to the house. Though part of the house was used up to 1973 by Mr. J. C. Graham, it is now unoccupied. The estate is now successfully farmed by his son, Mr. Campbell Graham.

37

38

39

37. CATTER HOUSE

Near Drymen Bridge on the Dumbarton Road, this Georgian style mansion was built in 1776, on the site of an old castle, for the Duke of Montrose's chamberlain (or factor).

It has an attractive curved two-way staircase

38. AT THE BRIDGE, DRYMEN

On the right is Mr. John Strachan, Sen., father of Mr. John Strachan, Drymen and grandfather of Mrs. Flora Holmes.

39. MR. JAMES TURNER, SENIOR AT DRYMEN SHOW

Drymen Show, instituted in 1816 by the 3rd Duke of Montrose, is one of the oldest one-day agricultural shows in Scotland.

leading to the front entrance. On private ground at Catter House is a large stone with a hole in the middle which supported the Earl of Lennox's gallows. Prior to the bridge being built in 1767 a ferry operated to take travellers across the Endrick when it was too deep to ford.

An iron turnstile and stone steps marked the place of crossing and can still be seen on the south bank of the Endrick, below the concrete fence.

On the left is Mr. Peter Atchison and behind the horse Mr. Duncan McGregor both helping him to take in his hay.

Getting a hurl on top of the load are Maureen Clyde, Rena and Betty Strachan, an evacuee (unnamed) and John and Mary Lamberton.

In the background right, is the old steading at Easter Catter, now gone.

Mr. Turner of Loaninghead Farm was well-known as an outstanding breeder of Ayrshire cattle. He is seen here with a group of five female Ayrshires, winners of their class in 1933.
Left to right: 'Loaninghead Pansy',
    Mr. J. Marshall,
    'May', 'Lady Bute',
    Mr. J. Turner, Sen.,
    'Jen', Mr. J. Turner, Jun.,
    'Lady Rachael' and Mr. W. Turner.

40. BUCHANAN AULD HOUSE

Also known as the Place of Buchanan and taken from a drawing by J. P. Neale, engraved by M. J. Barenger 1784. The mansion house and surrounding lands were owned by the Lairds of Buchanan from 1225 when a charter was granted by the Earl of Lennox to Maurice, Chief of the Buchanans.

When the last Laird of Buchanan died in 1681 the house and estate were bought by the third Marquis of Montrose whose family home at Montrose had been destroyed by fire. Buchanan House then became the principal seat of the Montrose family. In 1852 Buchanan House was almost completely destroyed by fire when the Duke and his family were in London for Christmas.

All that remained was part of a servants' wing at the rear. Buchanan Golf Clubhouse is built on part of the site of the old house.

41

41. BUCHANAN CASTLE FROM THE SOUTH

After Buchanan House was destroyed by fire the 4th Duke of Montrose had a new home built on higher ground nearby. By 1855 the family had moved into Buchanan Castle built of local grey sandstone in Scottish Baronial style.

The Castle and the Estate provided employment for large numbers of local people. The girls became domestic staff and the men and boys were employed as farm workers, joiners, masons, slaters, foresters, gardeners, gamekeepers, and after 1890, electricians. The Castle was the first house in the county to be lit by electricity, generated by turbines driven by the Mill Burn which flows through the grounds.

42

43

45

42. BUCHANAN SMITHY

The houses at Buchanan Smithy were built at the end of the 18th century by the 3rd Duke of Montrose for workers on the estate. In the 1800s Mr. David Mair was blacksmith, followed by his son-in-law Mr. Thomas Anderson, great grandfather of the present Mr. Tommy Anderson, Buchanan Smithy. Three generations ran the smiddy which had three blacksmiths at its busiest. It wound up about 1950 and for 35 years it was not used as a smiddy.

The appearance of the houses has changed little except for internal modernisation and for the last 8 years the Smithy has been the busy workshop of Mr. David Smith, a fine craftsman in metal.

43. THE BUCHANAN PLAYERS, 1952

Beside Buchanan School is the Memorial Hall built to honour those who died in the 1914-1918 War. It is used for many village activities including Sunday School, W.R.I. meetings, the men's recreation club, whist drives and the Annual Flower Show.

The Buchanan Players rehearsed and staged regular productions in it.

On the left are the cast of *Kye Among the Corn*, (a three-act play).

Back Row: Betty Bradford, Mrs. Annie Stewart, Neil Cairns, May Perryman (Mrs. Fraser), Jackie Cowie, Billy "Buff" Anderson, Donald Galbraith.
Front Row: Bill Pettett, Mrs. Mary Watson, Isobel Bradford (Mrs. Waddell) & Donald Johnson.

45. BUCHANAN PRIMARY SCHOOL 1957-58

Left to Right:
Back Row: E. Cameron, I. Cowie, D. Pettett, P. Melville, N. Ronald, C. Sellar, A. McIntyre, J. MacMillan, S. Forbes, A. Bayfield.

Front Row: J. Binnie, C. Adams, W. Love, N. Berry, M. MacMillan, A. Cairns, K. Roberts, R. McLaren, A. Berry, J. Vickers, V. Grainger, J. Bayfield.
The headteacher was Miss Ewing and her assistant Miss J. MacFarlane.

Starting back row, left: 2nd, Willie Ferguson, 3rd Dougie Campbell, 6th Peter Johnson, 7th Mr. John Dunlop (headmaster 1890-1918), 8th Jimmy Ewing, 9th Malcolm Downie, 11th Mary Dunn, 13th Jean MacFadyen, 16th Annie Penny, 17th Angus MacFadyen.

44

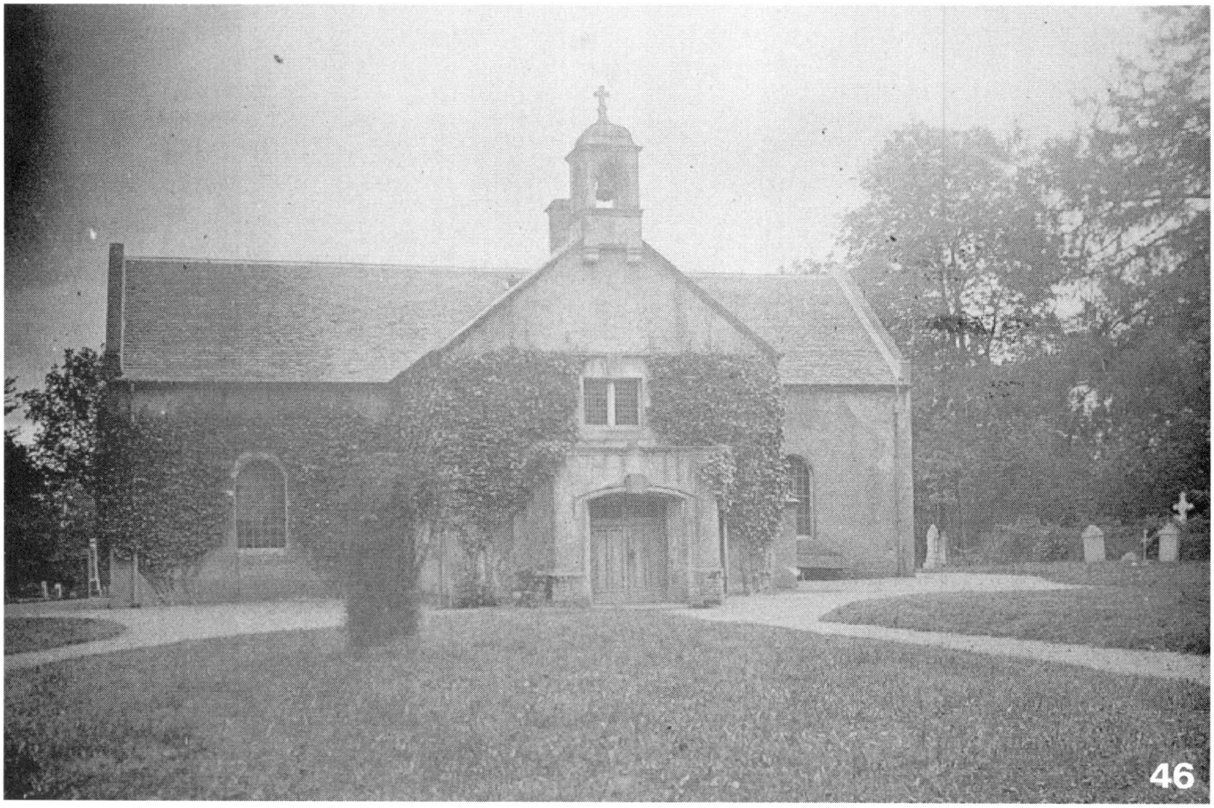
46

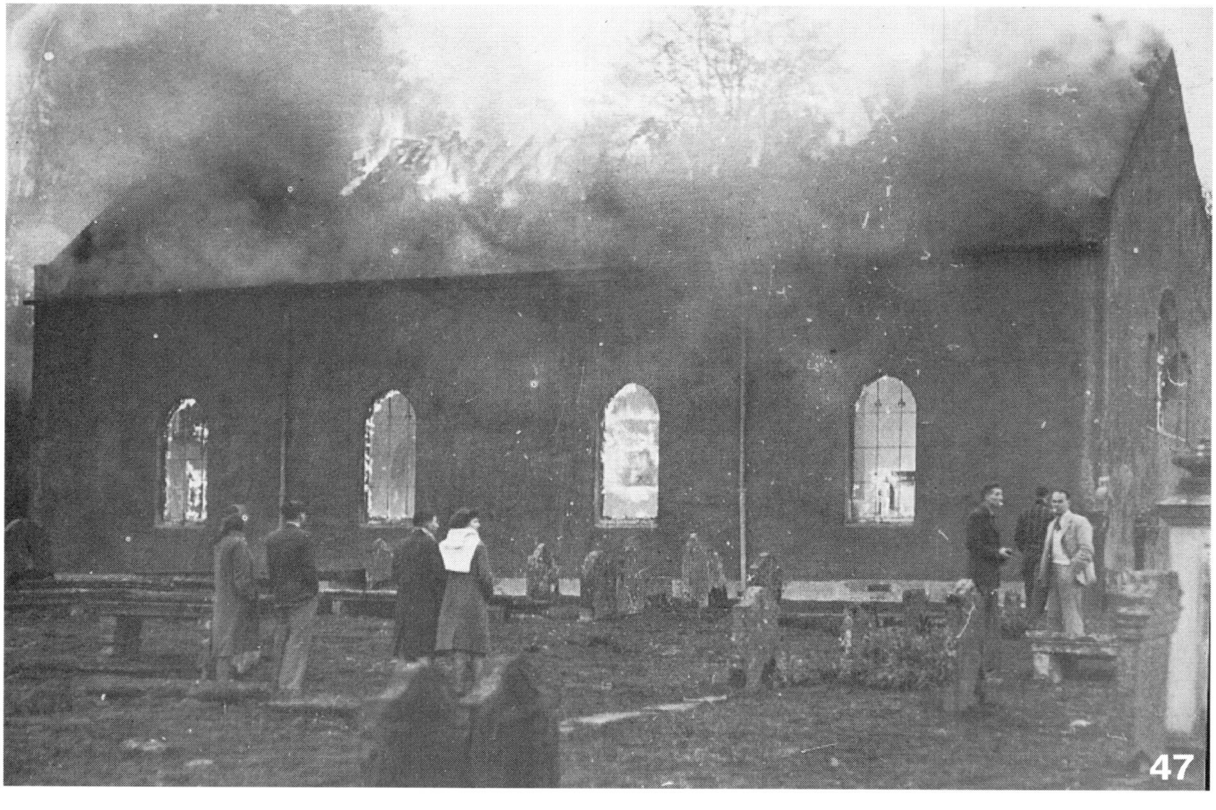
47

46. BUCHANAN PARISH CHURCH

The 3rd Duke of Montrose had this Church built in 1764 to replace St. Mary's Chapel at Buchanan Auld House which had been used as a place of worship since about 1670 when the original Church on the island of Inchcailloch had been abandoned. About this time the Parish of Inchcailloch was renamed Buchanan Parish.

This photograph was taken just before the First World War.

47. BUCHANAN PARISH CHURCH ON FIRE, 1938

The interior of the Church was destroyed by fire in May, 1938, said to have been caused by a faulty boiler.

Only the outer walls and the belfry were left standing. The stone font from the Church on Inchcailloch, one of the few remaining links, was lost in the fire. At the time the parishioners regarded the Church as finished but after little more than a year the interior was restored and in August 1939 was re-opened for worship mainly due to the efforts of the minister, the Rev. W. R. Lacey.

48. RE-DEDICATION OF BUCHANAN CHURCH, 1939

On 11th July, the above picture was taken when the re-building of the Church was completed.
Left to right: 1. Unnamed, 2. Mr. Donald Johnson, 3. Mr. Alex MacFarlane, 4. Mr. John MacFarlane, 5. The 6th Duke of Montrose, 6. Unnamed, 7. Mr. John Proctor, 8. Rev, R. D. E. Stevenson, Moderator of Dumbarton Presbytery, 9. Right Rev. Prof. Arch. Main, Moderator of the General Assembly, 10. Rev. J. T. Monteith, 11. Rev. W. R. Lacey, 12. Mr. W. MacLean, 13. Unnamed.

49

49. FUNERAL OF JAMES GRAHAM, 6TH DUKE OF MONTROSE

The coffin, draped in Graham tartan, was borne on a farm cart to the family burial ground in Buchanan Parish Churchyard on the 23rd January, 1954

Leading the horse:	A. Donaldson & A. Miller.
Behind the coffin:	W. Bradford, G. Watson, Unnamed, T. Ronald
Near pall-bearers:	F. Perryman, J. Proctor, J. Gilchrist, A. Hunter & A. J. MacFarlane
Following the Hearse:	R. Raeside, personal valet, carried the Duke's insignia and medals on a cushion; four members of the R.N.V.R., Angus, 7th Duke of Montrose; Lord Malise and Lord Elgin, representing the Queen.

The police officer is Mr. John Tait, Drymen.

50. REV. DR. AND MRS. WILLIAM MACINTOSH 1848–1892

He was described as an excellent preacher, a fine scholar and 'a thoroughly practical farmer', maintaining the Church, Manse and Glebe at Buchanan in good order. He also worked diligently in obtaining spiritual and educational benefits for all in the parish.

His forty-four years in the same Church was by no means the longest as both ministers and schoolmasters then devoted their lives to their parishes. Since 1764 when Buchanan Church was built there have been only eight ministers and at Drymen Parish Church seven, the Rev. W. J. R. Hay having been minister of both since 1981.

50

51

51. AN EARLY MOTOR CYCLE

Mr. James MacFarlane, uncle of the late Mr. Alex MacFarlane, on an early motor bike at Balmaha. He was electrician at Buchanan Castle.

52. THE "PRINCE EDWARD" AND THE "MAID OF THE LOCH".

The first paddle steamer on Loch Lomond was the wooden 'Marion' in 1817. After the first iron steamer in 1838, the numbers of paddle steamers increased rapidly and in the 1900s there were four ships on the Loch - Princess May, Princess Patricia, Prince George and Prince Edward. "Prince Edward" on the left was the largest ship that could be taken up the River Leven and plied the Loch between 1911 to 1955.

The 'Maid of the Loch' on the right was built in 1953 by A. & J. Inglis of Glasgow and was brought in sections by road to Balloch. This 500 ton paddle steamer sailed on Loch Lomond for 28 years and was the last of a fleet of steamers. For over ten years she has lain partly submerged and badly vandalised at berth at Balloch, her owners having gone into liquidation. It is hoped that the 'Maid' will be restored to sail again.

53. MR. ALEX MACFARLANE, POSTMAN

During the last 150 years, steamers on Loch Lomond have carried essential commodities to those living around the Loch and on the islands and also transported animals and wool to the markets. With the advent of the L.M.S. Railway those services declined, leaving the MacFarlane family who own the boatyard at Balmaha, as the main link with the islanders. In 1947 the late Mr. Alex MacFarlane became official postman and the photograph shows the Postmaster General for Scotland presenting him with his mailbag and contract to deliver mail daily to the islands. For the first time the 'Lady Jean' flew the Royal Mail Flag. His grandson Mr. Sandy MacFarlane carries on this unique service.

54

54. AT THE BACK OF THE PYROLIGNEOUS ACID WORKS, BALMAHA

The photograph may have been taken out of pride at the success of this Ayrshire cow at a local show. One hundred years later, the picture creates greater interest for the detail it gives of the back of the 'Liquor Works', showing the large water tanks fed from a nearby dam, now gone.

The acid distilled from oak, grown on the lochside, was used in the manufacture of dyestuffs for the printworks around Glasgow. Other products made from the distillation, were tar, creosote, methyl alcohol, acetone and acetic acid. The works whose origins went back to about the 1820s were owned by Messrs. Turnbull and Co. who also owned the Millburn Works on the River Leven (dating from 1806).

This picture is interesting also in that no houses had been built to the east (left of picture).

55

55. PETER JOHNSON AND 'TOMMY', 1903

Peter Johnson, grandfather of the late Donald Johnson, Milton of Buchanan was a carter for many years at the 'Work'. He lived at Passfoot Cottage where he died in 1913.

56. MR. GABRIEL FINDLAY AND FAMILY, 1903.

Mr. Findlay was manager of the Liquor Works for many years. He is pictured with his daughter Lucy (Mrs. Peter Johnson) and her sons Peter on the right and Findlay in the middle. Mr. Findlay died in 1905. The works continued until the early 1920s.

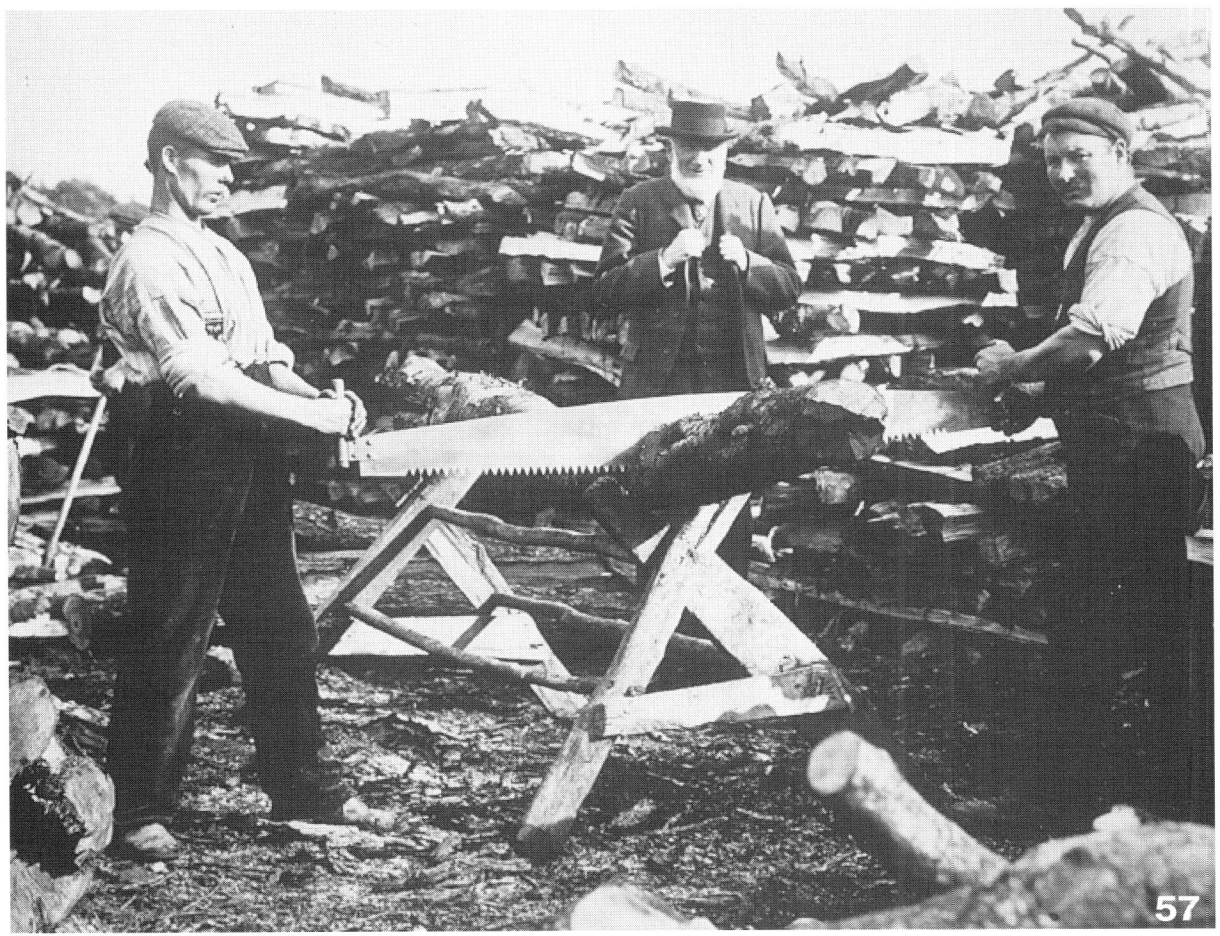

57. SAWING WOOD AT THE LIQUOR WORKS, 1903

Mr. Gabriel Findlay, manager, watches Tam Mackenzie and Peter Johnson (father of the late Donald Johnson), at work.

58. GROUP OF WORKMEN AT THE "WORK"

Left to Right

Back Row: Peter Johnson (he became manager at the age of 30). Man in bowler hat is a visiting chemist from Turnbull & Co., Camlachie, owners of the works, Tam Kilpatrick, Bob MacIntyre (fireman), Peter MacLean, a bricklayer from Camlachie (in white moleskins), George Henshilwood (postman).

Front Row: Johnny Campbell (with saw), Donald Johnson (younger brother of the manager), Tam MacKenzie, Peter Johnson (father of the manager), the child is his grandson, Peter. The man on the extreme left, the one seated on the extreme right and the small boy, make up three generations called Peter Johnson, the fourth, is the present Mr. Peter Johnson living at Milton of Buchanan.

58

59

59. AT SALLOCHY

Mr. David Wilkie, headmaster at Sallochy School is on the left.

By the middle of the 1700s harvesting oak for the tanning of leather had become a major industry in Buchanan Parish. The procedure used was called "coppicing". The woodland area, owned by the Duke of Montrose, was divided into 24 lots or "hags", each roughly 100 acres. There was a 24-year rotation and each year one hag was auctioned to a contractor. The bark was peeled and loaded on to flat-bottomed boats ("scows") and taken to Glasgow, Port Glasgow and Greenock. Some of the timber remaining after the bark-stripping was used to fence the recently felled area to protect the new shoots on the cut stumps from being eaten by domestic animals. The photograph shows the type of fencing made from small branches. The rest of the timber would be used at the liquor works, also to make charcoal, farm implements or be used as domestic fuel.

60

60. AT SALLOCHY SCHOOL, LOCH LOMOND

On the left is Mr. David Wilkie, headmaster at Sallochy. Seated is his brother, William, grandfather of the late Miss Nanette Wilkie, Hope House, Drymen. About 1726 there is a record of a Charity School being opened at Sallochy and this school remained in use until the mid 1920s.

When Mr. Wilkie the headmaster, decided in his seventies that he wished to retire, the School Board appointed a woman in his place. He refused to accept their decision and continued to teach while many strongly-worded letters passed to and fro. In the end he was forced to give up and Miss Mary Robertson took over.

61

61. AT THE CASHEL FARM, BALMAHA, 1879

Mr. John Scott, farmer with his shepherd and greyfaced tups.

Last century, the east side of Loch Lomond was more densely populated than now. From Church Session records in 1759 there were 58 families, totalling 262 persons, living between the Pass of Balmaha and Rowardennan. Previous to large scale planting by the Forestry Commission from 1931 onwards, the ruins of more than 30 crofts were to be seen in this area. Sheep-farming, the coppicing of oak, the slate quarry at Sallochy, iron-smelting, the distillery on Inchfad, forestry, and the Liquor Works would all give employment in the 18th and 19th centuries.

62

62. ROWARDENNAN HOTEL

From the end of the 17th century there was a drovers' inn at Rowardennan, the part on the right possibly being the original building. In Victorian times the hotel hired out ponies to take tourists to the top of Ben Lomond at 3,194 ft. Scotland's most southern 'Munro'. The hotel was sold about 1931 by the Montrose Estates and since then has had a number of owners, the present being Mr. & Mrs. Bob Nicoll.

This picture was taken by the famous 19th century photographer, George Washington Wilson. He toured the Scottish Highlands between 1850-1860 taking many photographs.